CAVE DETECTIVES

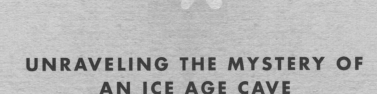

UNRAVELING THE MYSTERY OF AN ICE AGE CAVE

Written by David L. Harrison

Illustrated by Ashley Mims

Cave photographs by Edward Biamonte

chronicle books · san francisco

Permission to use the following photographs is gratefully acknowledged:
Front cover and pages 44–45: © Matt Forir; back cover, top right: © Lisa McCann; back cover, bottom
left: © Edward Biamonte; pages 4, 14, 18, 25, 27, 29, 30, 34, 36–38, 40, and 48 © Edward
Biamonte; page 10: © Harrington & Cortelyou, Inc.; page 12, top: © Bobby Page; page 12, bottom:
© Lisa McCann; page 16, top and bottom left: © Lisa McCann; page 16, bottom right: © Edward
Biamonte; pages 13, 17, and 20: © Lisa McCann; page 23, top: © Edward Biamonte; page 23, bottom:
© Lisa McCann; page 27, inset: © Lisa McCann; page 41, top left: © Sara Overstreet; page 41,
bottom left: © Lisa McCann; page 41, right: © Malissa Page.

Book design by Headcase Design.
Typeset in Futura.
The illustrations in this book were rendered with Luma watercolor dyes
and Caran D'Ache watercolor pencils.
Manufactured in China.

Library of Congress Cataloging in Publication Data
Harrison, David L. (David Lee), 1937-
Cave detectives : unraveling the mystery of an Ice Age cave / written by David L. Harrison.
p. cm.
ISBN 978-0-8118-5006-3

1. Caves—Missouri—Juvenile literature. 2. Speleology—Missouri—Juvenile literature.
3. Paleontology—Pleistocene—Juvenile literature. I. Title.
GB601.2.H369 2007
560'.17920977878—dc22
2005030067

10 9 8 7 6 5 4 3 2

Chronicle Books LLC
680 Second Street, San Francisco, California 94107

www.chroniclekids.com

For Sandy with love, for always being there, even in the cave.
—D. L. H.

ACKNOWLEDGMENTS

Many people played a role in the story of Riverbluff Cave. Their firsthand reports and advice helped make this a better book. I'm especially grateful to:

Jonathan Beard—cave specialist, editor of *MCKC Caving Journal*

Stacy Bergmann—road project engineer from Harrington & Cortelyou

Dave Coonrod—Greene County presiding commissioner

James Corsentino—cave mapper, explorer

Doug Eyman—Greene County Highway Department inspector

Matt Forir—paleontologist, lead scientist in Riverbluff exploration

Jim Francka—Greene County head inspector for road construction

Lisa McCann—member of Riverbluff exploration team

Bobby Page—blaster from Explosive Contractors

Jack Rowden—project manager, Journagan Construction

Randy Stewart—Journagan foreman for repair crew

Dr. Kenneth Thomson—geology professor, Missouri State University

Special thanks to Edward Biamonte, who spent three days in the cave taking many of the photographs in the book.

CONTENTS

• •

A LONG TIME AGO

BEFORE HUMANS ARRIVED IN NORTH AMERICA . . .

• •

A short-faced bear moves along a stream. He is a giant compared to any other bear that will ever live. He is mostly a carnivore, a meat eater. Whether he brings down his own prey, steals from smaller predators, or chases buzzards off a carcass, he is always hungry for meat.

The stream loops through scattered clusters of pine trees and crosses a clearing. It comes to the base of a hill and disappears into the mouth of a cave. The bear knows this cave. It is cool in summer, a good place to nap through cold winters, and a safe hideaway to nurture newborn cubs. Rolling his massive head, the bear enters the cave and vanishes into the darkness.

Sometime later a band of peccaries pauses outside the cave. The peccaries are about the size of pigs; they look much like pigs, too. For a while the peccaries mill around the entrance, snorting indecisively. When the leader heads inside, the others follow. Snuffling and grunting, the peccaries jostle one another down the black tunnel.

Somewhere beyond the light, the bear rises up from a deep pit. Without warning he strikes, his great claws slashing at the clay bank as he lunges toward the snuffling and grunting above him. Squealing peccaries flee in terror, but there is no escape. Even in the dark, the bear is deadly. He catches a peccary and bites its foot off. In a short time the killing ends. Silence returns to the darkness.

SEALED OFF FROM THE WORLD

• •

Many generations of bears come to the cave under the hill. Many other animals visit, too. Saber-toothed cats and American lions sometimes investigate the cave's dark tunnels. Dire wolves with bone-crushing teeth sniff the entrance.

Over time, the neighborhood around the cave is home to many animals, including mammoths and 6-ton mastodons, musk oxen and enormous ground sloths, armadillos and horses. When animals die, their bodies are usually eaten by scavengers until even their bones disappear. But sometimes their remains are washed away by floods and carried underground through cave openings and sinkholes. Most of the bones become buried under debris. Only a few clues stick out of the clay, proof that these creatures once lived.

Centuries pass and the earth's conditions gradually change. Temperatures become warmer. **Glaciers** that once covered much of North America start to melt. The cave is changing, too. Slowly, the openings to the cave fill in with debris. There comes a time when the great bears can no longer fit into the shrunken entrance. Not even peccaries can squeeze through. Finally, nothing can.

The cave is sealed off from the world. It is a tomb for the remains of unknown numbers of animals. Clay and stone build up inside the cave. For tens of thousands of years, water dripping from its ceiling goes unheard by any living thing.

UNCOVERING
A MYSTERY

· ·

The story you just read was pieced together thousands of years after it happened. How did scientists figure all this out? Clue by clue, much like detectives.

Before the road crew arrived

The story you are about read begins in September 2001, on a sunny day in the Midwest. Near Springfield in Greene County, Missouri, Journagan Construction is building a road. Bobby Page's job is to blow off part of a hill that is in the way. He and his crew get ready. Their hydraulic drill chatters down into the rocky earth, digging a series of small holes nearly 30 feet deep.

The crew places sticks of powder in the bottoms of the holes and covers them with ammonium nitrate, an explosive ingredient that looks like mayonnaise. The powder will set off the ammonium nitrate. Fuses and ignition caps are in place. A long line runs uphill to a place where the blast will be set off by the push of a button. People living nearby have been told there will be an explosion. Traffic on the road has been stopped to protect motorists.

Construction of the road

FIRE IN THE HOLE!

•••••••••••••••••••••••••••

Bobby raises his right hand, ready to call out the familiar warning. In another second, part of the hill will erupt. A geyser of dust and clay will shoot 30 feet toward the blue sky. A wave of shattered earth and stone will explode onto the roadbed. It will sound like a waterfall crashing onto rocks. Dust and smoke will swirl. The air will smell of burned powder like the stale remains of Fourth of July fireworks.

"Fire in the hole!"

The side of the hill explodes. Smoky clouds of dust and grit collide. But no wave of broken rocks crashes outward onto the roadbed. Instead, part of the hill vanishes into the earth.

Men scramble toward the blast site for a look. They stare down into a wide, jagged hole. The explosion has blown through the wall of a cave!

Driven by curiosity, Bobby picks his way down through the rubble. The floor is littered with slabs of rock that shattered off the ceiling. Bobby holds a lighter above his head. A few steps beyond the weak sunlight he finds himself in a dark, silent place. Wisely, he turns back. This unexpected cave is a serious problem for the road builders. It must be reported right away.

The explosion of the hill (top) reveals the cave (bottom)

Bobby looks inside the cave

DETECTIVES ON THE SCENE

· ·

What happens next shows just how much detective work is involved in cave science. When he learns about the cave, Dave Coonrod, the top Greene County official, notifies Ken Thomson, a **geologist** and cave expert. Ken identifies the rocks around this cave as **limestone**, a kind of rock that formed underwater when a shallow sea covered the area 360 million years ago.

Close-up of the limestone showing fossilized sea creatures

Ken Thomson can see that the newly discovered cave is big. It's hard to tell how far its tunnels might reach. He decides that it needs to be investigated. One of the first people he notifies is Matt Forir. Matt is a **paleontologist**, the kind of scientist who studies ancient life. Matt and team member Lisa McCann will be the first detectives to tackle the scientific mysteries of this unknown cave. They wonder if they are about to walk where no human has been, uncover secrets that no one has witnessed. They share a great responsibility, and they feel it.

"You can't be too careful," Matt says. "This may be just another cave. But there is always the possibility of finding priceless fossils that will help us understand what life was like in the past. A careless step might destroy something that can never be replaced."

HOW WAS RIVERBLUFF FORMED?

The main ingredients for this kind of cave are limestone, water, and time. Limestone begins as layers of mud, sand, silt, and clay that settle to the bottom of the sea. Mixed with these are the remains of trillions of plants and animals. Calcium from their shells and bones acts like cement binding the parts together.

Over time, layers of sediment grow thicker until the weight on top squeezes water from layers below and presses them into limestone rock. The seafloor may be pushed upward by movements deep inside the earth. When this happens the sea drains away, leaving the limestone exposed to the air.

Once exposed, the limestone immediately starts to break down. Then rain mixed with **carbon dioxide** breaks the limestone down further.

It takes a long time for this breakdown to happen, but bit by bit the cracks in the limestone grow bigger. Eventually they expand into tunnels. If a roof of a tunnel collapses in one part of a cave, the relentless water dissolves the pieces and washes them away, creating new passages, rooms, and chambers.

Geologists calculate that under normal conditions a cave may grow as slowly as 12 inches in 30,000 years. If Riverbluff Cave needed 30,000 years for each of its 2,200 feet, the cave could be 66 million years old. But guessing a cave's age is tricky. Estimates can be off by millions of years.

Surface water seeping into limestone slowly forms a cave

HOW DO CAVE FORMATIONS GROW?

The formations found in Riverbluff and many other caves are made mostly of **calcite**, which comes from the limestone rock that makes up a cave. As drops of acidic water enter the cave through cracks in its ceiling, they pick up small traces of calcite. When the drops evaporate, they leave tiny rings of calcite on the ceiling of the cave. Drop after drop adds to the rings, until slender strawlike structures form. Millions of drops later, the straws look more like icicles and are called **stalactites**.

Excess water drips to the floor, where new formations begin to grow. These are called **stalagmites**. Some stalagmites and stalactites grow together to form columns. Minerals in the cave or water add beautiful combinations of colors to the formations. Air currents can cause stalagmites and stalactites to grow into twisted patterns.

The formations inside Riverbluff

WALKING INTO THE PAST

● ●

Matt and Lisa work down through the debris and enter the blast opening. The first chamber of the cave is large and roughly round. The far walls and ceiling are only dimly visible in the lights mounted on their helmets. Stone formations of many shapes and colors hang from the ceiling and grow out of the floor.

Matt and Lisa edge forward. They walk between floor-to-ceiling columns that look like ice sculptures. Beyond the columns they pass a shallow pool so clear that the water is invisible. The floor slopes downward to the lip of a wide pit 10 feet deep and 30 feet across. The explorers slide down the slippery bank, wade through cold water above their ankles, and scramble up the far side.

Clay is everywhere. It coats the walls and the floor, and clings to their wet boots. One hundred feet into the cave, they stop to look at a wall. Their lights crisscross the darkness like narrow search-lights. Suddenly the beams come together on the same spot. Several feet above their heads, enormous claws have left deep slashes in the clay. Sometime in the past a living creature—a very large living creature—has visited the cave!

A STARTLING DISCOVERY

· ·

"**L**ook at the size!" Lisa says. The marks are 7 or 8 inches wide and 14 feet above the floor. That's 4 feet higher than a basketball hoop!

Matt's mind is already busy figuring out what kind of animal did this. "Bear," he says. But the only bear native to this area is the black bear, and black bears can't reach half this high. Their paws aren't more than 5 inches wide. The bear in here was a giant.

Matt feels a rush of excitement. "Only one kind of bear was ever big enough to make those marks," he says. "The short-faced bear. The one that autographed this wall stood here more than ten thousand years ago!" That's when the last ice age ended, and paleontologists believe that short-faced bears were already extinct by then.

As Matt and Lisa turn around, their lights shine on the far wall of the passage, picking up claw marks that look different from the bear claws marks. These scratches look like they were cut into the clay with knives.

Matt whistles. "Saber-toothed cat or American lion," he says. "This was a busy place!"

The explorers have only been in the cave for 30 minutes, but they return immediately to the surface. Matt's report to the others waiting near the entrance is simple and straightforward:

"We have to save this cave! You're not going to believe what's down there!"

The claw swipe of a saber-toothed cat or an American lion

WHEN WAS THE LAST ICE AGE?

Ice ages occur roughly every 100,000 years. The most recent one lasted about 70,000 to 80,000 years. At its peak, great sheets of ice covered nearly all of what is now Canada and much of today's United States. The first humans on this continent arrived during the later years of the most recent ice age, about the time short-faced bears were dying out. Our ancestors may have killed a few of those bears. Some of the bears may have dined on a few of our ancestors. Scientists track down all the clues they can about the most recent ice age because understanding that time period is key to understanding human development.

During ice ages, the world is covered in huge flat sheets of ice with distant peaks here and there

FOLLOWING A WATERY TRAIL

There are ponds, lakes, rivers, and waterfalls underground. In places where limestone is plentiful, miles of underground corridors, chambers, and pits carry tremendous volumes of water. This is especially true after heavy rains or melting snows flood the earth above and below the surface.

Lawn chemicals and fertilizers washed away by rain may flow through caves and show up again where least expected. If someone throws a dead animal into a sinkhole, the water it contaminates might travel miles underground. Because plants and animals depend on clean water, and because so much water moves below the surface, hydrologists study caves to track how and where water enters and leaves them.

Repairing the damage to the cave wall

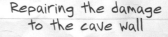

Damage inside the cave caused by the blast

SAVING THE CAVE

. . . .

County officials, Ken, Matt, and other scientists consult with the construction company and road engineers. They reach a major decision. They will reroute the road to one side to spare the cave. They name the cave Riverbluff.

A crew repairs the damaged cave wall with 20-foot sheets of ½-inch steel. The cave is buried again to keep it safe from intruders. Now it can only be entered by climbing down a 16-foot manhole and crawling through an underground drainpipe with padlocked steel doors at both ends.

By spring of 2002, the scientists are finally allowed to start exploring Riverbluff Cave. There is an air of excitement as they begin.

Mapping the cave is one of the first priorities. A map specialist named James Corsentino agrees to take on the task with help from Matt, Lisa, and other team members. "Crawling on your stomach through wet clay isn't always fun," says James, "but a good map is worth it."

Like explorers above ground, cave scientists need a map of where they're going. Geologists need to know the shape, size, and location of the cave to understand how it was formed. Paleontologists need to know where each discovery is made to understand what life was like in the area. **Hydrologists** (scientists who study water) need a good map to discover the role that water plays in the cave.

Scientists map the cave

FOSSIL FINDS

Exploration of Riverbluff Cave continues. Crew members spend many hours in the cave each week. Their careful work pays off. Not far from the big chamber they spot a round area hollowed out like a nest—a nest large enough to hold a bear. Now they realize that bears didn't just pass through this cave. At least one of them remained long enough to make a bed. What looks like lumps of clay scattered around the area are fossilized bear droppings.

The **fossil** of a snake skeleton lies a few feet away. This is another treasure for study. Above ground, fragile snake skeletons rarely survive long. Here in this protected place, these thin bones have lasted for thousands of years. Every discovery raises more questions. How far back into a cave would a bear and snake travel? Is there an entrance hidden nearby?

Matt discovers fossils inside the cave

Fossilized bear droppings

WHAT IS A FOSSIL?

Fossils often form when minerals in the surrounding soil and water slowly replace the body's original chemicals and leave a stone replica of the original object or animal. Soft tissues rarely survive long after death, so most fossils are shells, teeth, and bones.

Other fossils are imprints left in soft mud or clay. Over time the surface may harden, but in Riverbluff Cave the clay containing the claw marks is still as moist and sticky as it was when the impressions were made.

Fossils teach us many things. The animal droppings in Riverbluff are especially interesting. Bear and peccary droppings reveal the creatures' diets, including leaves, seeds, and pollen, that provide important clues about the soil, climate, and weather of that distant time.

Fossilized snake bones

LOOKING FOR A WAY IN OR OUT

• •

The scientists search for a hidden entrance to the cave. They follow a wide, low corridor that meanders slightly downhill. After 150 feet, what looks like an ancient channel dead-ends into gravel and rubble. The cave goes no farther in this direction. But the team believes that a stream once flowed out of the cave at this spot. There must have been an opening here large enough for snakes and even bears to use. If this was the exit, they should find the original entrance somewhere toward the other end of the cave.

Far into the north passage of Riverbluff, nearly 2,000 feet from the blocked-off exit, the explorers find what they seek—an ancient riverbed. No water flows in it now, but they can make out the channel where the river once ran.

They work their way forward with growing anticipation. The tunnel narrows. The ceiling drops until it scrapes the tops of their hard hats. Crawling on hands and knees, they trace the channel upstream, wondering if they will soon see daylight streaming into the darkness through a hidden entrance.

The riverbed stops at a wall, but gravel around the dead end matches gravel found outside in an old streambed that meanders toward the cave. James's map shows that this is the high end of the cave. Water would have to flow downhill from here and out through the exit Matt and his team found earlier. Another mystery is solved. What is now a sealed tomb was once a cave with openings at both ends.

Bear bed (left and above) not far from the original cave exit

MORE DISCOVERIES, MORE ANSWERS

● ●

The explorers are now 2,000 feet from the hole that the road crew blasted through the wall. At this end of the cave they come to a deep pit more than 40 feet wide. More bear claws—many of them—heavily scar the far bank of the pit clear up to the top where a narrow path runs along the edge.

Why did so many bears congregate here? For one thing, the pit is only 300 feet from the original entrance into the cave, so reaching this point would not have been hard to do. But why stop here?

Closer examination of the bank wall reveals that some of the prints are smaller and lower down, the way young cubs might have made their marks beside their mothers. Could this part of the cave have served as a nursery for the bears?

Sure enough, in a small chamber nearby, the team finds a cluster of bear beds. The ceiling here is so low that even Lisa, who is 5 feet 2 inches tall, has to pull herself through on her stomach. Lying near the lip of one of the beds, Matt makes a discovery.

"I found a bone!" he calls out to the rest of the team. The cramped space muffles his voice, but his excitement comes through. Wriggling out backward, Matt twists around to show the others the toe bone of a bear, the first bear bone found in the cave. This is a moment to savor. The date is July 19, 2002. Exploration of Riverbluff Cave has been going on for three months.

Still wondering what the bears could have been after on the trail above the bank, the team continues to examine the mysteries of Riverbluff Cave.

The claw marks of a short-faced bear.
Can you imagine how large its paws were?

SOMETHING NEVER SEEN BEFORE

Deep in the north passage investigators notice a long patch of clay that looks rough. Most other clay in the cave is smooth, unless something has tracked through it. Cautiously, as always, team members move in for a closer look. The clay is rough because it has been churned up by hard little hooves. Thousands of hoof prints run in both directions along one side of the tunnel. The tracks look fresh. Even the imprints of coarse hairs on the creatures' legs are plainly visible in the moist mud. These prints have lain here undisturbed since the creatures that made them disappeared into history. Piles of fossil droppings litter the runway.

"Amazing!" says Matt. "I think peccaries made these tracks. They were distant relatives of today's pigs. If I'm right, this gives us new information about the habits of these creatures. Their bones are fairly common in caves, but scientists have assumed that peccaries were dragged in by predators or their remains washed in. These guys walked 700 feet into total darkness on purpose!"

These peccary tracks look fresh but are thousands of years old

29

AN ANCIENT MYSTERY IS SOLVED

• •

If Matt is correct, this is a critical discovery. To verify that these really are peccary tracks, he plans to contact a peccary specialist in another part of the country to discuss this latest finding. But he is spared the trouble. A few hundred feet away, the team spots a small object in the clay. It is part of a peccary's foot. The bone has been severed from the body, snapped off by powerful jaws.

With this find, a mystery thousands of years old is solved. The bear claws on the wall and the peccary tracks in the clay suddenly become parts of the same story—the story you read in the beginning of this book. Looking at the severed foot, Matt and Lisa sit in silence. In this peaceful place they imagine the ambush in the dark and the explosive violence that erupted here so long ago.

Bones of a peccary foot bitten off by a bear

HOW LONG AGO?

How long ago did the bear kill the peccary? There are several ways to find out. Matt decides to start with **radiocarbon dating**. He sends bone samples from Riverbluff to a laboratory for testing.

How does radiocarbon dating work? Every living thing has a bit of radiocarbon (short for radioactive **carbon**) in it. After a plant or animal dies, it loses its **radioactivity** at a steady rate. Scientists can tell how old the remains of an organism are by measuring the radiocarbon it has left. It takes tens of thousands of years for an organism to lose most of its radiocarbon, but after 55,000 years, there's not enough radiocarbon left for an accurate measurement.

The radiocarbon test results come back from the laboratory. Matt expects the bear and peccary fossils to be 10,000 to 15,000 years old. That would place them toward the end of the last ice age and close to the time when both species became extinct.

But what he learns is that the test wouldn't work because the specimens didn't have enough radioactive carbon left in them to measure. The creatures in Riverbluff must have

For fossils older than 55,000 years, scientists can sometimes use a method called **cosmogenic dating**. This test is used on the soil surrounding the remains and measures how long ago the sun last shone on the soil. The results of cosmogenic dating can be accurate up to five million years or longer.

lived more than 55,000 years ago. They lived and died before the first human walked on the North American continent.

This news puts everything in a different light. The last ice age began about 90,000 years ago and ended 10,000 years ago. Instead of studying creatures from the end of that period, the scientists at Riverbluff are looking at much older history. They have an opportunity to learn more about life toward the middle of the ice age, maybe earlier. What should their next steps be?

Samples from this wall of the cave offer valuable information about the fossils buried in the clay

DIGGING DEEPER INTO THE PAST

· ·

Because the bear and peccary remains are too old to determine by radiocarbon dating, the scientists will have to try a different approach. Luckily, there are particles of **quartz** in the Riverbluff clay, so they're able to try cosmogenic dating. If the scientists can determine the age of the clay, they'll know the age of fossils found in the clay.

Matt studies the wall where he and Lisa discovered the original bear claw marks. When the ancient river came through here, its water slowly cut the floor deeper, leaving layers of clay exposed in the wall. The oldest layers should be toward the bottom.

Fossil bones of mammoth, horse, and musk oxen turn up in a layer of clay a few feet above the floor. None of these large creatures would have visited the cave while they were alive. Their bones either washed in or were carried in by predators. But when did this happen? If the claw marks toward the top of the wall are more than 55,000 years old, how old are these fossils lower down?

Scientists remove small squares of clay from the wall to study. They also drill holes several inches into layers of sediment. Each sample may contain tiny signs of ancient life, including pollen from plants that lived above ground at that time. The scientists prepare the samples for testing and send them off to be analyzed.

Pollen from ice age pine trees turn up in clay samples

NORTH AMERICA'S OLDEST ICE AGE CAVE!

• •

Once again, the research team is in for a surprise. Cosmogenic dating shows that the layer of clay where the mammoth bone was found is 630,000 years old. This is completely unexpected news. It means that the bones found in this layer rank among the oldest ice age fossils discovered in North America.

But that's not all. A core sample closer to the floor—containing pollen and other plant remains—is even more astonishing. The date goes back 830,000 years!

It is now 2005. Four years of patience, planning, exploring, and research have led to this moment. The information from the cosmogenic dating means that Riverbluff Cave is more than a fascinating treasure of old bones. It is one of the country's top caves

These circles are where samples were taken from the clay

for ice age research. This is a proud time for all who have been involved in discovering, saving, and studying Riverbluff Cave.

The news is announced across the nation. As cameras record the event, Matt encourages caution. "As of now," he says, "we think that Riverbluff is the oldest ice age cave fossil site in North America. Caves are discovered every week, and older fossil sites may be found, but Riverbluff has earned its place among the most important ice age discoveries on record."

An Ice Age discovery ha

DISCOVERIES CONTINUE

• •

Even as this book is being finished, Riverbluff continues to give up its secrets to careful observers. James Corsentino finishes his map. Or he thinks he has. We ask the crew to go back into the cave for a picture. They discover another 50 feet of passage. Someone drops a glove that disappears into a hole. Nicole, the newest team member, is lowered down into the hidden pit.

Is it a centipede or millipede?

"I think I've found something!" she calls up to the others.

Matt climbs down to see.

"This could be another first!" he says. "Looks like an extinct form of centipede or millipede. Either way it's a distant relative of insects."

Matt has never encountered fossils like these before. Judging from their location, he thinks they are very old.

How many other secrets lie hidden in this single cave, waiting for the sharp-eyed detectives of science? And how many other caves exist beneath our feet? Missouri alone has reported 6,000. Tennessee has 8,600 known caves. Kentucky has at least 3,700. Texas and Virginia have more than 4,000 caves each. Imagine an underground map of caves scattered across North America and around the world. Imagine all the information they hold about the past!

HOW LARGE ARE CAVES?

Riverbluff has 2,200 feet of passages, slightly less than half a mile. That is good-sized although not in the monster-cave category. Mammoth Cave in Kentucky includes 365 miles of passages and could be connected to other enormous systems that would more than double the total length. Several other caves in the United States and other countries twist and turn for 100 miles or more. Many have at least two levels, and some plunge deep into the earth. A cave in the country of Georgia (a neighbor of Russia) drops down more than 1 mile below the surface.

Matt and Lisa lower Nicole into a pit

THE ONGOING SEARCH FOR ANSWERS

· ·

We cannot change the past, but we can learn from it. One of the great unsolved mysteries for paleontologists is why so many animals died toward the end of the ice age. Again and again, important pieces to the puzzle turn up in caves.

It is not unusual for caves to be uncovered by construction crews building the nation's roadways. Most are destroyed or sealed over. If Riverbluff had suffered the same fate, the world would have lost a priceless storehouse of information about the past. Matt Forir believes that eventually the team will find fossils more than one million years old. It seems entirely possible.

THE RIVERBLUFF DETECTIVES

Lisa McCann and Matt Forir

Bobby Page

Matt, David Harrison, Ken Thomson, and James Corsentino

MORE ANIMALS OF RIVERBLUFF CAVE

• •

cientists believe that many different animals lived in and around Riverbluff Cave at one time or another. These are just a few.

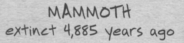

MAMMOTH
extinct 4,885 years ago

MASTODON
extinct 5,950 years ago

DIRE WOLF
extinct 7,500 years ago

EARLY HORSE
extinct 8,240 years ago

GIANT GROUND SLOTH
extinct 9,380 years ago

SABER-TOOTHED CAT
extinct 9,410 years ago

AMERICAN LION
extinct 10,370 years ago

WOODLAND MUSK OX
extinct 11,110 years ago

MORE FOSSILS OF RIVERBLUFF CAVE

· ·

These are some of the other animal fossils found inside Riverbluff.

Raccoon jawbone

Skunk jawbone

Horse bones

THE LIFE OF RIVERBLUFF CAVE

YEARS AGO	90,000	55,000	18,000	17,000
EVENT	Last ice age begins	Sometime before this a short-faced bear kills a peccary in Riverbluff	The peak of the ice age	North American musk oxen become extinct

YEARS AGO	9,410	9,380	7,500	5,950
EVENT	Saber-toothed cats and peccaries become extinct	Giant ground sloths become extinct	Dire wolves become extinct	American mastodons become extinct

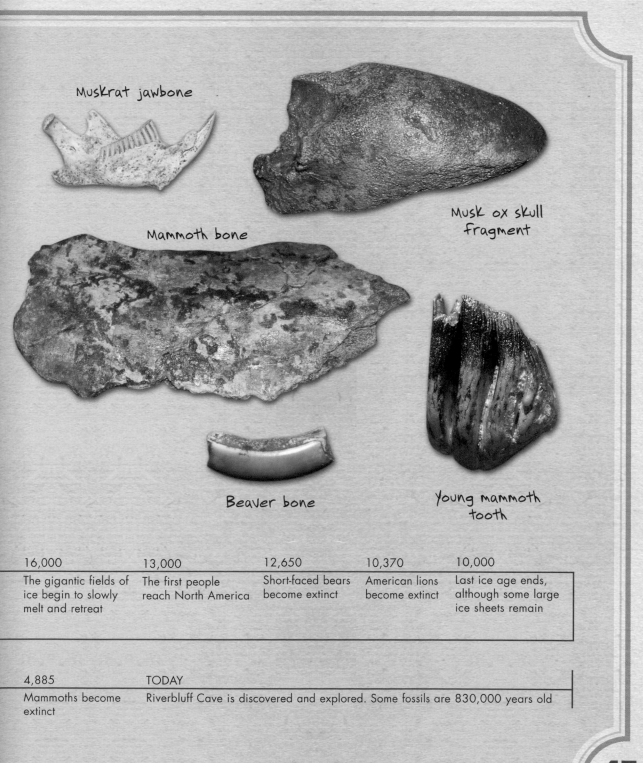

Muskrat jawbone

Musk ox skull fragment

Mammoth bone

Beaver bone

Young mammoth tooth

16,000	13,000	12,650	10,370	10,000
The gigantic fields of ice begin to slowly melt and retreat	The first people reach North America	Short-faced bears become extinct	American lions become extinct	Last ice age ends, although some large ice sheets remain

4,885	TODAY
Mammoths become extinct	Riverbluff Cave is discovered and explored. Some fossils are 830,000 years old

GLOSSARY

CALCITE: A mineral, also called calcium carbonate, found in limestone. Calcite is the basic material in most cave formations.

CARBON: One of the most abundant elements in the universe, found in diamonds, wood, coal, plants, and animals.

CARBON DIOXIDE: A colorless and odorless gas made of carbon and oxygen that humans breathe out and plants consume. Burning coal and gasoline releases carbon dioxide into the atmosphere and adds to global warming.

COSMOGENIC DATING: A method scientists use to determine how long ago sand was exposed to the sun by measuring the number of particles in quartz.

FOSSIL: Naturally preserved remains or evidence of ancient plant or animal such as a bone, shell, and impression.

GEOLOGIST: A scientist who studies the origin, structure, and physical nature of the earth.

GLACIER: A large, thick mass of ice and snow that moves down slopes or outward across level land, moving from a few inches to hundreds of feet per year.

HYDROLOGIST: A scientist who studies the distribution and movement of water, above ground and below it.

LIMESTONE: A common kind of sedimentary rock made mostly of calcium carbonate (calcite) from marine animals mixed with sediments (mud, silt, sand, clay) that settle to the bottom of a sea and become pressed into stone.

PALEONTOLOGIST: A scientist who studies forms of plants and animals that lived in ancient periods of history. Much understanding is gained by discovering and studying fossils.

QUARTZ: The most common mineral on Earth. It comes in many forms, shapes, and colors. Its two main ingredients are sand and oxygen.

RADIOACTIVITY: A chemical's ability to release energy as it breaks down.

RADIOCARBON DATING: A method of determining age by measuring the amount of radioactive carbon remaining in a specimen. Every 5,730 years, half of what's left is no longer radioactive. The test is accurate to about 55,000 years.

STALACTITE: A cave formation that hangs down like a stone icicle and is formed over time as millions of drops of water seep through cracks in the ceiling and evaporate, leaving behind small amounts of calcite.

STALAGMITE: A cave formation that grows upward toward the ceiling as calcite-rich drops of water drip onto the floor and evaporate.

ABOUT THE AUTHOR

David Harrison experienced his first cave at the age of four, sitting atop his father's shoulders. When he was twelve, he discovered an 8,000-year-old black bear skull in a cave near his home in Springfield, Missouri. By then his bedroom was filled with all sorts of rocks, minerals, and fossils. Today David holds a bachelor's degree in zoology from Drury University and a master's degree in parasitology—the study of parasites—from Emory University. He even has a 300-million-year-old fossil named after him! His lifelong love of caves continues—this is his third book on the subject. David and his wife Sandy have a daughter, Robin, a son, Jeff, and two grandsons, Kris and Tyler.